"Anyone can do a dog and cat comic, but Dawn puts undercover aliens studying the mysteries of humankind *inside* those animals. Now that's genius! Whether they're causing havoc in a typical office environment, commenting on the holidays or dealing with their own alien boss, Zorphbert & Fred consistently deliver the funny. With so many cookie-cutter comics on the web, Dawn's alien-inside-a-dog-costume point of view is a real fresh treat."

- Tom Dell'Aringa, *"Marooned"*

"Dawn Griffin has achieved the elusive trifecta of wonderful art, fun writing, and engaging characters. If you want a solid newspaper-style comic with modern sensibilities and great gags, look no further than Zorphbert and Fred."

- Tony Piro, *"Calamities of Nature"*

"Dawn Griffin's entertaining comic strip milks plenty of laughs out of the cleverly simple concept of using two aliens (disguised-as-dogs) as a way to comment on the world around us.

- Bob Pendarvis, Sequential Art Professor and publisher and co-editor of SUGAR NINJAS, an all-girls comics art anthology

"Holy &^%$, a bit of the twisted wonderfulness of life in a beautifully drawn comic. A webcomic that came out of the womb kicking @$$."

- Jennie Breeden, *"The Devil's Panties"*

"Zorphbert & Fred is one of those rare comics that can be read and enjoyed by anyone in the family. I love Dawn's ability to tell a fantasy story but still pull in everyday life references! You rock, Dawn! There, I didn't even make fun of you…"

-W. Byron Wilkins, *"1997 The Comic"*

ZORPHBERT & FRED

VOLUME ONE: PREPARE TO BE ANALYZED

By Dawn Griffin

to Liam!

you humans are WEIRD!

THIS BOOK IS DEDICATED TO:

My father Dennis- head xerox-er of my first submissions.

My sister Marybeth- anal editor in chief and tracker of all typos.

my mother Martha- life-long supporter and fellow creative work-horse.

My grandfather Floyd- gadget man and closet artist.

More than anything, I want to thank all the wonderful readers that have willingly jumped on the Z&F train, and ridden with me over these first three years. Your emails, your comments, your overall support of my life's dream to draw funny pictures for a living is irreplaceable. It's what makes this field amazing, and what keeps me going, when it's three hours past my bedtime and the coffee maker is broke.

Extra-special thanks to John McCarthy and my sister Marybeth Griffin for helping me edit this book!

FORWARD
BY TOM RACINE OF "TALL TALE RADIO" PODCAST
www.talltaleradio.com

I believe in love at first sight, because I have seen "Zorphbert and Fred." If you're a fan of the classic comics page, you'll find a home as soon as you start experiencing the world Dawn Griffin has created. The characters all have unique voices and personalities, and like all great comics, you can see that in their very character design, attitudes and poses, without a word being spoken. Dawn is a great cartoonist, and the detail she puts in her work is so refreshing in the world of webcomics, which can get way too simplified for my tastes. Don't take my word for it... you've got the proof in your hands.

The history of webcomics, if it can even be called that yet, is mostly filled with sci-fi geek strips, computer programming humor, and fantasy and video game strips. But Dawn has found a way to bring in her obvious love of such things into a strip that could fit in any newspaper anywhere, and to cover topics that range through the whole human experience. She's chosen a conceit that is an endless source of amusement... the oddball antics of the human race as viewed by visiting aliens. WE can barely understand ourselves... what chance do aliens disguised as dogs have? (Actually, come to think of it, my money's on the aliens.)

One of the things I love about the webcomics revolution is that it has given voice to so many amazing female writers and artists out there, and Dawn is in that upper echelon of creators. There's been a ridiculous bias against females in comedy since the beginning of time it seems, but Dawn can bring the funny with the best of 'em, male or female. You can tell by her meticulous care in the writing that she works very hard at finding the humor, the joke, the timing, the pathos, and the heart of every one of her strips. "Z&F" hit the ground running and just gets better and better. Maybe it's the zen guy in me, but the best thing about Dawn being a "female cartoonist" is that it never enters your mind, because you're too busy laughing at the strip. All you see is the "cartoonist" part.

And if there are nicer creators to support and follow, I haven't met them! "Zorphbert and Fred" is one of the best stops on the web for your comic cravings."

INTRODUCTION:

So, hi. I think introductions are hard to write for most creators. There's the dilemma of writing it in first-person and sounding like a conceited idiot, or writing it in third-person and sounding like a pretentious conceited idiot. Do you get sappy and ramble on about dreams and callings and passions? Or do you play it cool, make it a comedy routine about all your rejection letters and embarrassing moments? Well, here's the facts: I'm a cartoonist, and this is the first Zorphbert and Fred collection. I am also a graphic designer for a snack foods company and kid's book illustrator. And a Cleveland sports fan. And a dog owner. And a lover of ice cream. But nonetheless, I still have to write something about THIS BOOK. Focus, Dawn, focus.

I wouldn't say the idea behind Zorphbert and Fred "came out of nowhere". There were no singing angels and golden beams shining down from above one quiet evening. It was a long process of brainstorming, borrowing concepts from comics, TV shows, movies, animated series, and other mediums that inspired the basic idea. I wanted it be something *unique*. The fact that I had retired my previous strip, "Leftovers," leaving me a gaping hole in my life, gave me the kick in the tush to just sit down and sketch, write, conceptualize, and just run with it... wherever it took me.

Z&F's basic idea stemmed from the 90's sitcom "Third Rock From the Sun"– as goofy as it could be, the way these characters saw humankind, and all the weird little things we take for granted (like, sneezing, or Jell-O), really hit home with me. I think once in a while, we all feel like aliens on this planet, separate from the grind of civilization and wondering about the big picture. That's where I want Z&F to take the reader: to that mind-set. The interaction between Zorphbert and Fred is the result of an age-old character combination: that of Garfield & Odie, of Bucky & Satchel, of Laurel and Hardy. This comic duo teeters on the line between played-out and timeless, I hope I can achieve the latter.

It all comes down to one thing, really. Comic strips are the one medium that fully showcases all my strengths: drawing, storytelling, humor, organization and dedication.

I hope you enjoy this book.

Ah yes, the very first strip. The strip where I told myself, "Enough of this endless brainstorming about how this comic should start, just friggin' WRITE."

I don't think I have ever shown either of the dogs scratching since this strip. Which is kinda odd, 'cuz dogs scratch. Like, a lot.

One of the books I read on how to train your dog, suggested using the phrase, *"Do your business"* when teaching your dog to go in the yard. Imagining someone following their dog around the yard saying *"Do your business, Rover! Do your Business!"* amuses me to no end.

Some people ask me if Fred is gay since he wishes to be dressed as a cat. But even then, that would make Fred a wanna-be cross dresser, not gay necessarily. But, can aliens BE gay anyway? Straight? Now I'm confused, so stop asking me that question.

This is still one of my ultimate favorites. That's saying something; because usually after a year, I hate it.
On another note, though I tried my hand at marker in the first 4 strips, this is where I started adding tones in Photoshop.

I guess I just like toying with the idea that Fred could be gay? Just run with it.... I have been.

Zorphbert has repeatedly said "Freddie, my boy". I like the quasi-stuffy British element it bring to Zorphie's character. Although, when I hear his voice in my head, it doesn't have a British accent, so go figure.

Although I enjoy Fred's thought process here, I'm not a huge fan of this punch line.

Anyone remember that cartoon short "Family Dog"? It was a spinoff from Steven Spielberg's "Amazing Stories", created by the now famous Brad Bird. The gross dog food panel was inspired by one episode of that short series.

Zorphbert may have a point. Excuse me, my dog wants to go outside...

This entire strip may very well have been written solely to use the phrase "peon scum". Yes... yes, I think it was.

The first glimpse of the elusive tentacle!

Do you know how sick I was of drawing that basket by this point?

Tummy rubs are universal.

This is one of those strips that progresses the story line, but isn't that funny. I take solace in that every cartoonist I know has done one of these at SOME point.

I love drawing Fred from behind. His big plump tush is so cute. I'll just say it: fat characters are more fun to draw than skinny ones.

Another position I have never drawn Fred in since this strip. If he were alive, I'll bet he'd thank me, too.

Wordy, wordy wordy. One of my biggest criticisms of my own writing. I make the excuse that part of Zorphbert's character is to be long-winded and complicated... but not sure how long I can run with that.

They should consider themselves lucky. I know very few people, including myself, who built a doghouse for their dog. Actually, I think it's just a myth, used in cartoons and sitcoms.

Fred's smile in the third panel cracks me up. I call it the *"Christmas Story Smile"*, a la Ralphie as he asks Santa for the Red Rider gun. It must come with a pause in dialogue to qualify.

Overdone gag, I know... but it still amuses me; probably because of the whole Fred-Gay thing.

My very first memory is looking up at the curtains in my bedroom- white, with the Peanuts characters all over them. That was it, really... just a photograph in my mind. I thought I needed to work in a tribute to my first inspiration- Charles Schulz.

This comic was "Remix-ed" by a fellow "Ducker" on drunkduck.com, a webcomics community I belong to. Comic Remix is a community project where people redraw others work anonymously, and in return, the same is done for you. It was a fun project.

Remember when I said after one year I tend to hate some of the work I've done? This is one of 'em.

Also not a big fan of this one anymore, but I had to introduce the Squirrel manager somehow.

I intended to carry on the supposed "mind control" powers Zorphbert has, but it seemed to fall by the wayside over time.

See my exciting experimentation with sound effect fonts? Everyone: "OOOOOOO....AHHHH....."

Zorphie doesn't like being called "Zorphie". But seriously, no one can SAY "Zorphbert".

More of Zorphbert being wordy. Good thing Fred's there to lay it out for you in layman's terms.

It's true I modeled the human owners after myself and my (now) fiancé, but not every detail is true to life. We are BOTH into sports and BOTH pretty geeky. Good, now things are all cleared up.
P.S. Holy Wordiness, Batman! (see? geeky.)

Love the simple gimmick of not seeing the whole picture until the end.

Another over-done joke... actually, I tried to cram in a second one, since I thought the first one wasn't good enough. Bill Amend pulls that off well in Fox Trot. Not me, though. This one is just weak. My apologies, just turn the page already.

Get it? Strays? Orphans? Ha ha... oh, nevermind.

The introduction of the "Weird Kid", a now favorite character. Most describe him as a grown up Calvin from "Calvin and Hobbes".... if Calvin sniffed glue and was on all sorts of ADD drugs. I needed a human character that could interact with the aliens; and the glue-sniffer kid is just the type that would actually see that they are aliens.

I know I'm the one who wrote it, but I am very curious as to what happened in the "Adopt a Plutonian Incident".

Talk about an imagination that runs away with itself. I like writing for the Weird Kid, I just do a brain purge, and whatever comes out is probably just fine.

Another favorite of mine. "Frisk him for Ritalin and Pez" is a great line. *Pats self on back*

That's right, I worked in a Mr. T quote. What? ....WHAT?

This was one of those strips that I thought was pretty weak at the time, but I got a decent response to it. Every cartoonist seems to have these strips... which proves just how subjective humor can be.

In early 2007, I completed about 40 odd strips and was preparing for a syndicate submission. I wanted to post them online to look more professional, and gave drunkduck.com a shot. Two weeks later, to my surprise, Z&F was front-page featured. The first panel was the image selected as the "featured" icon.

Soooooo glad my managers and supervisors don't have warping technology to appear behind me at work.

Ahhhh yes, the introduction of the beloved "sock tail". Fred is now a Drag Queen. But ain't he cute? That second panel drawing of him is one of my favorites.

Cats are just weird. The purring, the kneading, the falling-on-all-fours, the "butt-switch" that sends their rear end into the air if you pet their back... it freaks me out.

The elusive and ever-difficult text-free comic strip. Harder to do than you may think. A good cop-out: use pictures in the balloons instead of words. No one will notice.

Another sub-plot I wanted to reuse was the "merit token". I had all sorts of ideas that involved the idea of biscuits becoming "badges of honor" for the guys. Alas, it was put on the back burner, and.. well.. burned. Maybe I can bring it back.

This is a perfect strip to me. It's a simple concept, has good timing and progression, it makes the reader curious about the final outcome, and hey!--- it's not too wordy!

I am not one to touch on politics too often, but this strip has been criticized for being too preachy- making my bias known. I guess that's a bad thing. I am hoping to be more of a George Carlin: no one is off limits. But I do have my biases, and it's hard NOT to use my comic as an outlet sometimes.

Like the "fetch" comic, I also think this one was well done. The "3rd panel pause" is another tactic I use often and it works excellently here. Poor Fred.

I'm sorry, but how can one NOT laugh at butt-sniffing?

Nettika is introduced. In retrospect however, she should have not have been as surprised as she was upon seeing Zorphbert. Oh well, hindsight.

Oh yeah, Nettika's a "Precious" *something*, alright...

I use the word "twit" a lot. It's one of those words that says exactly what it means. I named a pet rat "twit" once. I bet you feel as though you met my pet rat, huh?

Fred's final line is a poke at the Todd Goldman "Boys are stupid, throw rocks at them!" controversy, which was followed by the Godlman-David Kelly "Dear God Make Everyone Die" plagiarism. It very much dates this strip, and if you're not huge into this stuff anyway.... well, nevermind this whole comment.

Sopranos. Also dates this strip.

This was another comic that was "Remix-ed". Please see the end of this book for more.

I had originally thought this strip was forced and overdone, but got a lot of good feedback about it. You never can tell, I suppose. It's nice to see some interaction between the humans and the ~~dogs~~ aliens, though.

Wow. Anna Nicole's baby and K-Fed? It took me THIS LONG to put out a book?

Fun Facts: my favorite movie theater candy is Snowcaps. Now, wasn't that fun?

Zorphbert teases us with his mind-control powers again. I believe this was the last time it was mentioned.

You know why I love comics? Characters can just magically attain items from nowhere and no one questions how or why. Thus, the magic sock tail.

I must have debated over the shiny object in the trash can for nearly 2 hours. I certainly hope a whistle is the most hilariously perfect object that could be in said trash can.

This strip must have been written during my "Whose Line is it Anyway?" obsession. The funniest thing on TV I have ever seen was when Richard Simmons guest starred. Yes, THE Richard Simmons. Yes, in the full glitter work-out outfit. It was bring-a-tear-to-your-eye amazing.

It's the weirdos who are shockingly normal, and the normal people who are closet-weirdos. That's some deep philosophical thinkin', right there.

Man, this one was fun to draw.

I used to love the old York Peppermint Patty commercials. Those and the Klondike commercials; the ongoing theme always made you wonder what they were gonna come up with next. Now, I'm glad there's digital cable and DVR, so I can fast-forward through the commercials.

The final line in this was not written by me. It was submitted by a friend from drunkduck, Tom Potter, and I chose it over others' suggestions. It was the beginning of what would become the "Put Words in Their Mouths" Caption Contest. More on this later in the book.

I love this one. The big dramatic third panel that gets fizzled in the end, by a game of Go Fish.

A small tribute to "Pinky and the Brain" from The Animaniacs in that first panel. And oh yeah, is it just me, or does everyone immediately think of Richard Gere when a gerbil is mentioned? I know it was proven false and all... but the myth lives on.

This is another one of those politically preachy strips I probably shouldn't have done, but C'mon... "NU-CU-LAR"?! Really?

Oh yeah, and while I'm at it, a strip on religion. Might as well get them out of my system.

Another of my weaker ones.

Exploitation is okay as long as there's food involved. Lesson learned everyone?

This was the first real Caption Contest I ran. Another "drunkduck-er", Chris Ciancanelli, won the contest; he wrote this entire comic! As I continued with this contest, I started keeping it separate from the comic, so the rest will be shown the "Bonus Material" section of my books.

Here's one of my more bizarre short story lines. It went over well. I think surreal weirdness resonates with my readers.

I have to admit it was fun drawing "Fat Nettika" and "extra-frumpy Fred".

aaaah ha ha ha. The old Fred-could-be-gay joke. Never gets old.

More tentacles! The question I get the most is if I'll ever show the aliens without their costumes. And I always reference "Home Improvement'"s Wilson, face hidden behind the fence. Cheesey as the show was, the gimmick was funny. Plus, my interpretation of an alien will never beat that of your own imagination.

I remember driving around with friends in late high school, bored out of our minds, and making up point systems for pedestrians we could hit. Kids on bikes got you 5. The elderly were only 1, easy to hit. However, feisty elderly with walkers were 5 for comedic value, and nuns.. well.. nuns got you 10. Not that we ever implemented it of course.

Have to give the credit to the writers of "Emperor's New Groove" for the "No Touchy!" line. One of the best underrated Disney flicks.

... and thus ends one bizarre little story.

... and we pick up another bizarre story! Jumpin' right back on the horse!
I like this one a lot. The idea that one of Earth's products could be used for something entirely different on another planet is goofy... yet not too crazy enough that you couldn't consider it, just for a second.

I hope I don't get sued by Spam® over this Spam® Bath story line. Of course, it would make a great story, to say I was sued by Spam® over a dinky comic strip. Then I could write about my experiences in dealing with a Spam® lawsuit. Rinse, repeat.

Maybe Fred could be Spam®'s new mascot, "Spam® Boy". Maybe that would be enough to call off the lawsuit.

My apologies to women everywhere dealing with PMS at this very moment. Nettika said the Jabba line, not me. I have chocolate.... don't hurt me.

I think I did a good job with the "sniffing action shot". It's the small things.

Y'know, everyone likes a good squeaky toy now and again. I love the gestures and expressions in this one, makes me want to animate a Z&F cartoon one day.

yeah... not a fan of this one anymore.

I often wonder, as I watch with envy as my dog lies sleeping in the sun as I work, if my dog is really BORED OUT OF HER MIND.

I know it's a minor detail, but it bugs me that I screwed up the proportions of Z&F in the last panel. Fred is supposed to be quite bigger than Zorphbert. This comic begins what was my longest running storyline thus far.

I find it amusing that even with their superior technology, teleporters still come with big dusty printed manuals.

I think I have referred to "Planet Nurf" a couple times in the strip. During my brainstorming sessions prior to writing the first Z&F strips, I was trying to pin down a little of the aliens' history, including their home planet's name. "Nurf" was what I came up with.

Zorphbert's hand motions in the last panel are what saves this comic.

This one is sooooo busy. But I think it still works.

In the past few years, Zombies have become the new fad in webcomics. Not sure how these things happen, but hopefully I'll be around still when "alien dogs" get hot.

And suddenly, Fred's costume has pockets! I love comics.

I guess this is my "environmental/ Z&F Go Green" comic. Or, my anti-bus comic. Either way, let the hate mail roll in.

And so I introduce another character that can "see" aliens for what they really are. These human characters all have one similar trait: outcasts from society. And both the Weird Kid and homeless guy have, um, vices.

This one's a little racy for Z&F, but I think I pulled it off well. It became an instant favorite with some readers.

This was comic #100. A typical tradition for the drunkduck community is to include their devoted reader's characters in a landmark comic. Thus the insanity that ensues, here.

When in doubt, use alien technology as a punch line.

I've been dying to do some office humor. Z&F is no Dilbert, but it's fun to compare technology levels.

I'm glad I do not work in a cubicle. My art department is like a big shared room, full of toys and knickknacks and other weird stuff.

I still giggle at Fred chewing his paw in the last panel. Add this one to my top 20.

I do not deal with clients much at work, so if I get a phone call, it's probably the receptionist telling me my food was delivered. Still, the most exciting phone call of the day.

A pet peeve of mine at work. Man, make more dang coffee if you finish it, it ain't that hard.

Zorphbert has a multitude of handy gadgets that he can whop outta nowhere. He's like my grandfather.

Again, I wrote it.. but I have to wonder what "THAT" substance Fred mentioned is.... eesh.

There's a part of me that's so Fred (like here, I have done this before), but some days I can really act like Zorphie as well.

That poor guy is still in the bathroom.

In this first telelporter story, I had decided that the guys would teleport from doghouse to doghouse, as a means to sustain a "point A" and "point B". However, this got to be tedious- having to always write a "traveling" strip where they find their "warp point". Thus, later I created a handheld teleportation device, leading back to their doghouse.

I caught this very episode of the 700 Club one morning and wrote this strip that evening. I think people take things way too seriously sometimes. Besides, what kid dresses up as ghosts and goblins anymore? It's all spiderman and princesses now.

Another of my top 20 favs. If you note the bucket on Zorphie's head, you'll see a reference to my hometown football team, the Cleveland Browns.

Unfortunately, this is not too far off from my own living room during a Cleveland game. This is why my fiancé won't watch games with me anymore. "Uncle! Uncle!" I took from *A Christmas Story*, though I'm sure this wasn't only a quote from that movie. But it's the only place I've heard it used.

Readers seemed to love the "NO SNOT" box. Sometimes it's the little details people latch on to.

My dog loves leaves. I have even trained her to dive into the pile when I say "go get the leaves!". It's hilarious. She's the same way with snow, actually.

"Cahoots" was one of those words I log away in a notebook, for the sole purpose to write a strip around it. Another one I have logged away: *persnickety*.

I toyed with that last line FOREVER. I'm still not 100% happy with it.

The word play in this one was well done I think. Sure is true to my thanksgivings.

Even Fred is fooled by "archaic Earth technology."

Tetris is one of my all-time favorite video games. It's the game (along with Dr. Mario) that got my mom hooked on video games, and my Nintendo. I find if you play it for too long, you start seeing Tetris shapes in everything. This is the only time I ever showed the world through the cut-out eyes of the aliens' costumes. I should do it more.

How many people can say they drew a snowman's butt crack? Another fine achievement by yours truly.

Another attempt of mine at a non-text comic. Again, with the picture bubbles.

Bringing the outside, inside. Christmas time must seem very odd to outsiders.

I am going to go on record as a complete dork and tell you that this was one of my mom's favorites.

Ahhh.. the disinterested "confetti toss". I often wish I had a handy packet of confetti to randomly toss when others are waaaay more excited about some mundane event than I am. "OMG, Dawn! It's time for the *Survivor* marathon!" .....*confetti*

Who doesn't love the Wii? Or Wii-related webcomics? There are quite the over-abundance of 'em.

This about sums up my experience with jogging. And salads, for that matter.

I went through a low-carb diet a while back. It's amazing how much food is crossed off your list when you go low-carb. I suppose because most of the easy-to-make dishes and grab-and-go foods have breads, pasta, or the like. I'll go on record saying that it sure didn't work for me. All it did was hike up my cholesterol.

"Dough Boy" came from "The Drew Carey Show", it was Mimi's "pet name" for Drew. Being from Cleveland, I have to like that show.

I used to play basketball... a LOT.. in high school. And every practice we had to go through the hell that is *Suicides*. Between those, and the up-and-down-the-stairs running, I just about died every week. No one ever asked, "Why are they called "suicides?", that's for sure.

I still admire my "WHUMP". It's a good "WHUMP".
....That sounded weird.

Had to quote Ellen Page from "Juno".... she brought back the word "kudos" for me. I even implemented her specific emphasis on the word, too. Thank you, Ellen. Like she'll ever read this.

I enjoyed freaking out the Squirrel Manager with the Weird Kid. I figured I should have the two meet at some point. As a sidenote, I'd like to visit the "Suspended Sanity Chamber" one day, it'd probably be a blast.

This is not the first time I drew the Squirrel Manager on the Weird Kid's head. If you recall, that's how he saved Z&F from the Weird Kid in his introductory story. Must have amused me.

The dude sniffs glue. I'd be scared too.

If you note the name of the high school, it was a reference to a friend's comic, "Pugnuggle Tales", with the main character of that same name.

The phrase "Packin' crayons" still cracks me up. But seriously, the idea of guns in grade schools is pretty scary.

I cannot recall a locker I had that I could ever fit into. Nor do I remember anyone I knew being shut into one. I think it's another myth, like doghouses.

Fred, deep down you know you're a "snooga", so just deal with it.

Man, nothing is worse than being picked last, not to mention being argued over... because you are just that bad. I wasn't always an athlete, I recall my days of dodgeball and kickball being pretty miserable.

There's not a lot of scenes that are more fun to draw than food fights. Something else I think is a myth, I have never seen a food fight or been apart of one. At least not one of this scale.

Never had a desire to taste glue, though I do remember a kid in my class who did eat it (NOT a myth!). Sniffing markers was another "kid vice", and I had markers that smelled like the flavor they were marked- cherry, blueberry, etc. Wonder if mothers ever sued that company for their kid's brain damage.

Note Fred's "A Christmas Story" smile. Always funny.

Don't think I portrayed that last panel as well as what I saw in my head. Complex way of saying "I biffed it."

Guess the Weird Kid doesn't need a dose of that gas... or any 10 year old boy for that matter, really.

Wait 'til ya see what he does at 4:00.

Oh yes, baseball. I like the sport, I used to play it, but I do not blame anyone who finds it excruciatingly boring to watch. But in the mid-90's, was I ever glued to the TV for the Indians' 2 trips to the World Series (lost both). My family even drove back to Cleveland from Philly, to.... *drumroll* ....watch the game at an old neighbor's house.

The "low watt bulb" joke is one I have used for years. It needed to be put in a strip before I spontaneously self-combusted.

More wii jokes! The console is just fuel for us cartoonists. So many possibilities.
P.S. Fred liking Oprah does not (necessarily) mean he's gay.

Comin' at ya with the celebrity-name puns now! Can you handle it?

I like this one simply for all the different angles I used. In a comics world of talking-heads, I'm glad I can pull this off.

Love me some Guitar Hero. I'm no pro at it (nor am I musically gifted at all), but when you finally nail a song in that game, it's a pretty good feeling. My parents not only own the Wii (that in itself is not surprising for them), but I got my mom into Guitar Hero. Now that's impressive.

Hate to admit that I do not actually own an Atari 2600. All I have is the plug-in-and-play Atari controller with 20 games. However, that little $20 device has "Adventure" on it, which was my all-time favorite Atari game ever. You're the little square, find the keys, open the castles, avoid the dragons that look like ducks. Fun times.

My genius brainstorm session for this comic:
1. Look around the room
2. Write a comic about the first object you see.

"Cheesy Poofs" are the crack of the snack food world. But there are so many kinds: the small crunchy cheeto, the big poofy styrofoam kind, and my ultimate favorite... the small, twisty, melt-in-your-mouth kind. We had a brand of these in Cleveland, but they are not sold here in Philly. I have to stock up when I travel back to the midwest.

One of the few times I had to resort to the "wanna make sure you get this" arrow and descriptor. Hate it.

I don't do silhouettes nearly enough as I should. I like them.

Am I wrong or is "NOM NOM NOM" like the bestest sound effect to ever come from the internets?

Such as life as a teenager in New Jersey in the 90's. The choices were: A: Diner (where the waitress is sick of serving you *just* coffee for 3 hours), B: mall (please, we all hated the mall.) or C: go see whatever movie looks like it reeks the least.

Wow, their "Accessory Feature" is totally hip, yo.

I once read an article about just how terrible movie theater food is for you. I will pretend I never read it. Pass the nachos.

Hey look! The Third Panel Pause! I never do that!

If you are wondering, NO, that is not what Zorphbert and Fred look like under their costumes.

Ironically enough, I think money is rarely what my fiancé and I argue about. We're both broke and can't afford anything, what's to argue about? I just figured it's the typical couple argument.

I am often accused of "going off the deep end". I won't deny that, but at least I don't bring up "Armageddon".

There's a "Men are From Mars, My Dogs are From Venus" joke in there somewhere. I just know it.

This strip got criticized for being sexist, insinuating that men should always apologize whether they are right or wrong. I didn't intend it that way, but I do think a lot of men don't know what else to do... maybe because their wives don't just tell them what to do. Dang it, I think that came out sexist again.

After the last strip, I tried to be sympathetic towards the male character here. Not sure if I succeeded with that.

We had a BBQ once, the first big one where we invited half the block over for burgers and dogs. It was also the first time firing up a secondhand grill. Needless to say, no one had a problem finding our house; just follow the billowing smoke.

For some reason, I love drawing the ~~dogs~~ aliens sitting in a baby pool.... their little feet poking up out of the water. Dawwwww.

Usually, the formula for a typical Z&F strip is this: Zorphie sets the story, Fred does something innocently cute, Zorphie makes sarcastic remark, Fred sadly says something even cuter. That's why this one is refreshing... Zorphie doesn't even react to the baseball gear mishap.

If you are a baseball fan, you will have no doubts as to why I picked this matchup.

I am pretty proud of that last panel, I have to say.

Borrowed from a George Carlin joke, where he compared football to baseball. R.I.P, George. Don't come back to haunt me over this, k?

I have no idea how I come up with these weird alien names. Even "Zorphbert", I cannot tell you how or where or why I came up with that. Maybe it sounded like "Norbert" and that seemed formal and British enough for his character. But that's just me B.S.-ing.

I've always wanted to shoot one of those hot dog/tshirt guns. It seems like such fun.

I must be the only dork alive that still enjoys the wave. I find it hilarious when the crowd boos the other sections for not keeping it up. "Screw the game we paid to see, stand up on cue and scream! Now that's fun!"

If the story is just getting good, throw in the Weird Kid to make it even better!

I love Fred's comment in the final panel. Still makes me giggle.

Fred, the Snack Food Warrior! Coming to a ballpark near you!

Dang proud of my Sportscenter interpretation in the last panel. I actually dug up pictures via Google images so I could get it as accurate as possible. Though they probably have changed their TV set since.

Am I the only one who finds seeing mascots on breaks, smoking or drinking, highly amusing? Like, more so than whatever the mascots do normally?

Nothing like a beer hat on an animal to add some comedic value.

Yeah, I might very well have seen a firefly outside and immediately wrote this comic, too.

It may not translate in grayscale very well, but yeah... that's a rainbow in the third panel. Use your imagination. It is very pretty.

I hate hate hate yard work.
Hate. Yard work.
Is it obvious?

This reminds me of a scene in Disney's "Sword in the Stone." Merlin's pet owl, Archimedes, shakes himself off after being in the water and he puffs out in dramatic fashion. I thought it so funny as a kid that I would rewind it and play it over and over. His line, "Gollllly FLUFF", only made it that much funnier. Sounds lame now, but just trust me. Fuuuuuuuuuu-nny.

You know what would be HILARIOUS? Zorphie in a baby bonnet. Gee, I'll just have to write a strip around that.

I got my hair cut. Thus, my character had to get hers cut. Otherwise, nothing would make sense. The world would spin off its axis and everything on the planet would cease to exit. Deep end? What deep end?

Some doggy treats at the pet store really freak me out.

Well... what OTHER sound effect do you think flippers would make?

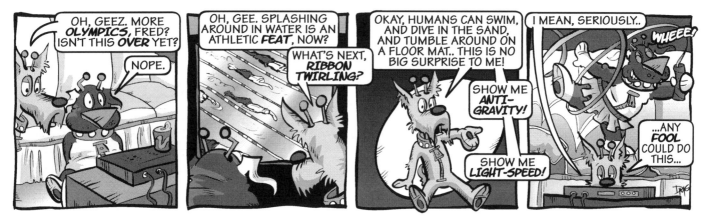

Phelps was an outstanding athlete in these Olympics, yes, but in the end... he's just splashing around in the water. I'm sure he'll appreciate that.

Sorry, Detroit readers, but as someone from Cleveland.... it's your friggin' turn.

I know it's just a goofy comic strip, but sometimes I feel the need to dissect advanced technology like the teleporter, and explain exhaustively how it works... for those hard-core sci-fi people who may complain.

Don't ya just love to see the conceited know-it-alls FAIL with fantastic grandeur? *snickers*

Despite their tiny little frames and chipmunk voices, I always envisioned gymnasts to be nasty little divas behind the scenes. Not sure where that comes from.

Everyone has those slow-to-process friends.... and you often wish you had a stopwatch to prove it.

Classic Zorphbert-- cumbersome and wordy. Still dig that 2nd panel, there's a lot going on, but it's represented well.

Oh, good old reliable naive Fred.

This was the very first "Sunday" strip I did, and it's still my favorite of the long-formatted comics. "Space Invaders" holds a place in my heart from my childhood, and it was also my dad's favorite game. He would play it before work, while he was waiting for the bus to come. Also, "Herb" is a great uncle name. Everyone should have an Uncle Herb.

Paddle ball is the most inane, boring toy. Even as a kid I remember "not getting it." However, at every block party, dozens of punching balls were passed out, and THAT was hours of fun. Go figure.
(for those who don't know, a punching ball is a like a thick balloon with an elastic loop, that you bounce annoyingly off your hand... much to the dismay of adults in ear shot.)

This is probably the only time I have shown Z&F with a toddler. I should do "baby-sitting" comics more, I think they offer a whole slew of new ideas.

Obviously, a hometown tribute. And, coincidentally, even the handheld teleporter doesn't know what or where Cleveland is. Ohio, folks. Cleveland is in Ohio. Yes, people still live there.

AND NOW FOR SOMETHING A LITTLE DIFFERENT...

Hey, if you've made it this far: THANKS.
Now, my loyal readers, we come to the REAL reason you purchased this book:
The extra-special bells and whistles that make up the BONUS MATERIAL!
(everyone: ooooooo, ahhhhh!)

I realize that the webcomics industry is a little odd. I mean, we artists give you our work for FREE online, and then ask you to purchase what you already read in book form. Lots of you fine readers DO (and we appreciate it!), and that's why it has become a little so-called "Industry". The idea that people make a living off their webcomics is amazing to me... it's taken me a while to get my head around the no-syndicate-no-newspaper route, as that's all I have ever known. So, anyway, this section is my little *Thank You,* to all you supporters, readers, fans and friends who have helped me along the way, even if all you did was buy this book. I hope you enjoy it... and find some solace in buying something you could have, well...
*....already read for free *wink wink**

THE BIRTH OF ZORPHBERT AND FRED
SKETCHES FROM A LONG, LONG TIME AGO

Here are some initial sketches from 2006 and 2007, as I got to know the characters. Note Zorphbert's floppy ears, Fred's white snout, and how much smaller both their noses were. Fred's crooked antennae switched too. It's amazing how fast they grow *sniff*

THE BIRTH OF ZORPHBERT AND FRED
CREATION AND EVOLUTION

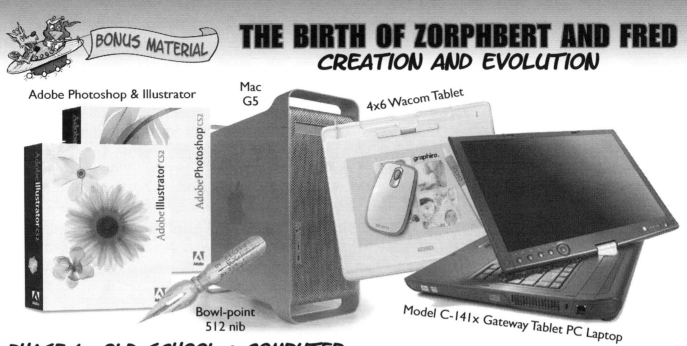

Adobe Photoshop & Illustrator

Mac G5

4x6 Wacom Tablet

Bowl-point 512 nib

Model C-141x Gateway Tablet PC Laptop

PHASE 1: OLD SCHOOL + COMPUTER

Out of college, I picked up where I left off on my old comic strip "Leftovers." My technique consisted of pencil sketches, fountain pen and ink for the lineart. the color and text was added in Photoshop after the lineart was scanned in. Using a Mac G5, I worked mostly in Photoshop CS2. I fine-tuned the process by setting up the panels on 8.5_11, 2 by 2 (2 panels on top, 2 on the bottom) for easier scanning. This meant I circumvented having to patch together multiple scans- quite the pain in the butt. I kept the lineart on one layer and colored beneath it on another layer using a mouse and the paintbrush tool-- which was quite tedious. However, this process worked well for a long time.

PHASE 2: THE WACOM TABLET

In my second year of Z&F, I decided to give this new-fangled wacom tablet thingy a whirl. My hope was that I could work on comics 100% digitally… Save time on scanning, cleaning up in PS, waiting for ink to dry, etc. However, I found the disconnect of looking at the screen while drawing on the tablet sucked the enjoyment of inking right out of the process. I was able to train myself to ink, but not sketch. I still sketched with pencil on paper, scanned it, and inked digitally. Around this time I also switched from Photoshop to Illustrator. I found that I could get a clean, slick line in Illustrator using vector brushes, whereas Photoshop lineart often had a slight roughness to it that I disliked. It was a good way to dip my toe into the possibilities of what technology can offer me as a cartoonist.

PHASE 3: THE GATEWAY TABLET LAPTOP

For my birthday in August 2008, from my generous mother and grandfather, I received a Gateway Tablet PC- model C-141x with a 14" screen to be exact. Yes, you draw directly on the screen and the tablet is wacom-enabled-- which means it's pressure sensitive like the Wacom tablet itself. Works seamlessly with Photoshop or Illustrator. You may wonder why I "choose" this over the ever popular Cintiq tablet. The answer: portability and price, my friends. This is also a fully functioning laptop that I can take anywhere. Now, for you Mac Heads, you may be thinking: "UGHHH! WINDOWS! EVIL! RUN AWAY! RUN WAY!". While I prefer the Mac, I also know Windows has come a long way in leveling out the discrepancy between how Adobe products run on a Mac and on a PC, and I have little against the general usability of a Windows OS (also looking forward to upgrading to Windows 7.) So, now my process is very simple. Sketch, ink, color and add text, all on the Gateway Tablet PC. Generally, although it may not be for everyone, this machine is exactly what I need.

1. First, draw rectangles for the head and body.

Then add in triangular shapes on top of the head for ears, and another for the snout.

2. Then, add ovals for the eyes, on the head.

Tack on an oval about the same size, but horizontal, for the nose.

More ovals for the paws, and use simple lines to lay-out where the legs will go. Don't forget the cylinder for the collar on the neck!

3. Add angular lines for tufts of fur on the ears, by the neck and under the snout.

Create the cut-out eyes with 2 double-ovals, and structure the legs, adding the toe lines to the paws.

Add circles & sticks for the antennae, collar circles, and the zipper!

4. With the pencil sketch done, ink over it with a thin marker or fountain pen.

I use thick lines for shadowed areas, or places where I need emphasis, and thin lines for gentle features. My signature element is the hatch lines, which I use to show shadows, texture, or depth.

BONUS MATERIAL

1. Fred's head and body are both oblong ovals, pudgier at the bottom, and more pointed at the top.

His body is usually almost double the size of his head.

2. Add Fred's nose. It's a triangle, the top part being longer and almost stretching across his face. Leave room for his mouth below.

Draw ovals for his feet. Fred usually sits upright, on his tush. Draw in some pudgy arms, and wavy ears, almost at the top of his pointy head.

3. Add in the accessories: the collar, the sticks and circles that make the antennae, the toes and the oval on the bottom of the feet. Draw the zipper like a curved ladder.

The mouth starts from the bottom of the nose and curves out. Add 2 double-ovals for the cut-out eyes!

4. With the pencil sketch done, ink over it with a thin marker or fountain pen.

I use thick lines for shadowed areas, or places where I need emphasis, and thin lines for gentle features. My signature element is the hatch lines, which I use to show shadows, texture, or depth.

117

"PUT WORDS IN THEIR MOUTHS"
CONTEST WINNERS

Back in my Drunk Duck days, I wanted to find a way to really interact with my audience. After all, immediate feedback and community support are what makes webcomics so special. I came up with this *"Put Words in Their Mouths"* Caption Contest for two reasons. A: to allow readers to become a bigger part of the Z&F universe, and B: to give myself (and probably my bout of Writer's Block) a much-needed break from writing funny stuff. The premise was simple: I draw a simple concept with blank bubbles, and entrants will offer their scripts and I pick my favorite one. The result was a lot of fun and I was often shocked at how big a turnout I received in way of entries. Of course, I also had to bribe people to play by offering the prize of a cameo appearance in the next Z&F strip-- of either the winner's own characters, or of the winner him/herself in cartoon form. There's nothing more exciting for a cartoonist than seeing how other cartoonists draw your characters. The following are the winning captions and the cameo prizes.

Written by: James Zintel   **Comic:** Gary & Ted   **URL:** www.garyandted.com

"PUT WORDS IN THEIR MOUTHS"
CONTEST WINNERS

Written by: Dan McMahan   **Comic:** Bucket Gnome
URL: www.bucketgnome.com

Written by: Erik Hodson   **Comic:** Chad The Fat Kid
URL: www.drunkduck.com/Chad_the_Fat_Kid

"PUT WORDS IN THEIR MOUTHS"
CONTEST WINNERS

Written by:
John H Midgley
Comic:
Blood/Hound
URL: www.drunkduck.com/bloodhound

Written by:
Steve "Spang" Rowles
Comic:
The Gods of ArrKelaan
URL: www.rmcomics.com

"PUT WORDS IN THEIR MOUTHS"
CONTEST WINNERS

MERRY CHRISTMAS, YOU TWO.

WONDERFUL. EARTHEN FIRE FECES.

A STARBUCKS GIFT CARD! SWEET CARAMEL MACCHIATO *HERE I COME!*

HONEY, IF YOU THINK I'M WEARING THIS *COLLAR,* YOU'RE NUTS.

Written by: Brock Heasley **Comic:** The Superfogeys
URL: www.superfogeys.com

THIS IS OUR GERBIL, HE WAS A GIFT FROM *RICHARD GERE.* WANNA HOLD HIM FRED?

PUT IT DOWN! *PUT IT DOWN!*

I'VE HEARD OF THIS RICHARD GERE AND I KNOW WHAT HE DOES WITH *THOSE!*

AWWW, WHEN YOU SAID "RICHARD GERE", HE GOT THE *CUTEST* LITTLE LOOK ON HIS FACE!

Written by: Frank Jordan **Comic:** Company Man
URL: www.companymancomic.com

"PUT WORDS IN THEIR MOUTHS"
CONTEST WINNERS

Written by: Dan Mehlhorn   **Comic:** Morning Squirtz   **URL:** www.morningsquirtz.com

"PUT WORDS IN THEIR MOUTHS"
CONTEST WINNERS

Written by: Steve "Spang" Rowles
Comic: The Gods of ArrKelaan
URL: www.rmcomics.com

Written by: Tom Potter   **Comic:** Zombies Are People Too
URL: www.drunkduck.com/Zombies_Are_People_Too

"PUT WORDS IN THEIR MOUTHS"
CONTEST WINNERS

JUST WHEN I ALMOST HAVE **YOU** TRAINED ON THE TELEPORTER, THEY GET **ANOTHER** ONE THAT REQUIRES **TRAINING!**

Written by: Corey Dye
Comic: Raw Fish
URL: www.drunkduck.com/Raw_Fish

Note: This one was special, as Rick and I just adopted a dog from a shelter that week. Thus, I had to include "April" in this contest. However, this was just a suspended idea, the owners did not actually get a third dog. Later in the comic, I developed a puppy character living next door based on our April, to further annoy Z&F.

HERE YA GUYS GO... A REAL BALL-PARK FAVORITE... **HOT DOGS!**

CRACK!

YIPES!

THAT BALL IS COMING STRAIGHT FOR US! PROTECT YOUR **WIENERS!!!**

BONK

SOMEHOW I DON'T THINK THAT'S WHAT HE WAS TALKING ABOUT, FRED.

Written by: Chris Ciancanelli   **Comics:** Confetti Surprise / Untold Tale of Clerks
URL: www.drunkduck.com/Confetti_Surprise_Volume_One / www.drunkduck.com/Untold_Tales_of_Clerks

"PUT WORDS IN THEIR MOUTHS"
CONTEST WINNERS

Written by: Kelly Ferguson **Comic:** Basketcase **URL:** www.basketcasecomix.com

"PUT WORDS IN THEIR MOUTHS"
CONTEST WINNERS

Written by: Dan Mehlhorn   **Comic:** Morning Squirtz   **URL:** www.morningsquirtz.com

"PUT WORDS IN THEIR MOUTHS"
CAMEO PRIZES

"ZORPHBERT AND FRED" *Featuring "Gary" from "Gary & Ted"* by Dawn Griffin

Winner: James Zintel   **Comic:** Gary & Ted   **URL:** www.garyandted.com
Another fellow alien webcomic writer, James' off-the-wall humor is always good for a laugh, or at least a raised eyebrow. Or a shake of the head. Either way, that crazy alien is always up to something.

"ZORPHBERT AND FRED" *Featuring "Dan" from "Dan The Man"* by Dawn Griffin

Winner: Dan McMahan   **Comic:** Bucket Gnome   **URL:** www.bucketgnome.com
Back on drunkduck, Dan did a comic called "Dan The Man", about a Charlie-Brown type main character, who never gets a break. He has since moved on to "Bucket Gnome", a cute little comic about a pygmy troll, and well.. a gnome with bucket.

"ZORPHBERT AND FRED" *Featuring "Chad" and other characters from "Chad The Fat Kid"* by Dawn Griffin

Winner: Erik Hodson **Comic:** Chad The Fat Kid **URL:** www.drunkduck.com/Chad_the_Fat_Kid

In the midst of the "City Excursion" story line, I had to incorporate a cameo of the acne-covered teenagers of "Chad The Fat Kid". Once I realized that a lot of the teenage politics we remember still exist once you're working in an office, it was an easy undertaking.

"ZORPHBERT AND FRED" *featuring Gwen from "It's Hard Out There For a Gwen"* **by Dawn Griffin**

Winner: John H Midgley **Comic:** Blood/Hound **URL:** www.drunkduck.com/bloodhound

John is the brains behind the fantasy/sci-fi-esque webcomic Blood/Hound, but in his spare time he wrote an adorable photo comic featuring his very own daughter, Gwen.... using all those classic "begging for a caption" kid pictures!

"PUT WORDS IN THEIR MOUTHS"
CAMEO PRIZES

"ZORPHBERT AND FRED" *Featuring "Ronson" from "Gods of Arr-Kelaan"* **by Dawn Griffin**

Winner: Steve "Spang" Rowles **Comic:** The Gods of ArrKelaan **URL:** www.rmcomics.com

"The Gods of ArrKelaan" is one of the longest running and most popular webcomics on Drunk Duck. It features the adventures of the bitter and lovelorn God, Ronson (the God of alcohol, obviously). When Steve and co-creator/brother Chuck posted this cameo, Z&F had one of its biggest traffic days ever! Thanks guys!

"ZORPHBERT AND FRED" *Featuring Captain Spectacular & Swifty (and more) from "The SuperFogeys"* **by Dawn Griffin**

Winner: Brock Heasley **Comic:** The Superfogeys **URL:** www.superfogeys.com

Brock and I "grew up together" on Drunk Duck, so we both got to see the other's work mature and move on to bigger and better things. Drawing his spunky retired "Superfogeys" was a blast, and I still love the irony of elderly "action" figures.

"PUT WORDS IN THEIR MOUTHS"
CAMEO PRIZES

"ZORPHBERT AND FRED" *Featuring characters from "Slim Red Ninja" and "Dan The Man"* **by Dawn Griffin**

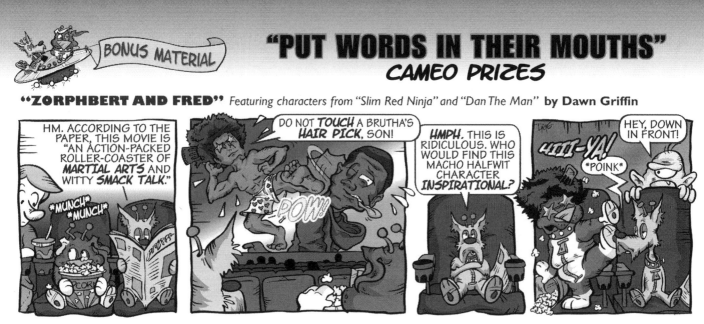

Winner: Dan Mehlhorn **Comic:** Morning Squirtz **URL:** www.morningsquirtz.com

Winner: Dan McMahan **Comic:** Bucket Gnome **URL:** www.bucketgnome.com

A rare incident where I could not chose between 2 entries. So, two Dan M.'s won, one the brains behind a funky pro-fro action webcomic, and the other a previous winner and drawer of gnomes.

"ZORPHBERT AND FRED" *Featuring Ron and "Old Bob" from "Company Man"* **by Dawn Griffin**

Winner: Frank Jordan **Comic:** Company Man **URL:** www.companymancomic.com

Frank's "Company Man" is the pop-culture zanier version of "Dilbert". When I discovered, this "Old Bob", who mainly drools and positions his eyes as above, I had to make him Weird Kid's father. It's an obvious move.

"PUT WORDS IN THEIR MOUTHS"
CAMEO PRIZES

"ZORPHBERT AND FRED" *Featuring "Thor" and "Isurus" from "Gods of Arr-Kelaan"* **by Dawn Griffin**

Winner: Steve "Spang" Rowles   **Comic:** The Gods of ArrKelaan   **URL:** www.rmcomics.com
Another repeat winner, Steve's other godly characters are tossed in Z&F's world, in a pick-up game of basketball. I have a feeling this was around the time of the NBA playoffs, and my Cavaliers were in the running. Basketball on the brain, for sure.

"ZORPHBERT AND FRED" *Featuring Jay & Silent Bob from "Untold Tales of Clerks"* **by Dawn Griffin**

Winner: Chris Ciancanelli   **Comics:** Confetti Surprise / Untold Tale of Clerks
URL: www.drunkduck.com/Confetti_Surprise_Volume_One / www.drunkduck.com/Untold_Tales_of_Clerks
Chris was a nonstop force on Drunk Duck, whether in making the controversial and always edgy "Confetti Surprise", or whipping up more tales for Kevin Smith's rowdy characters to partake... and the dynamic between "Jay and Silent Bob" is not too different from 2 familiar alien-dogs we know.

"PUT WORDS IN THEIR MOUTHS"
CAMEO PRIZES

"ZORPHBERT AND FRED" *Featuring the 2 Zombies from "Zombies Are People Too"* **by Dawn Griffin**

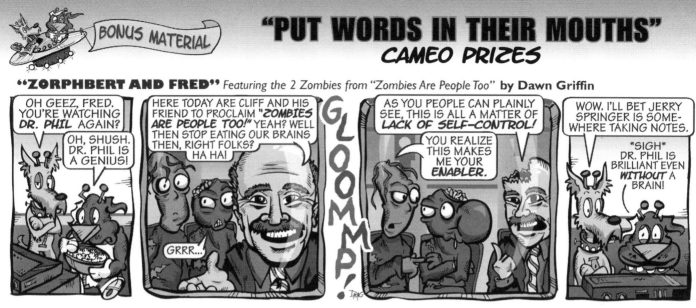

Written by: Tom Potter   **Comic:** Zombies Are People Too   **URL:** www.drunkduck.com/Zombies_Are_People_Too
Zombies seem to be a big fad in webcomics as of late, but this one by Tom Potter put an offbeat spin on the typical Zombie horror comic... by making them funny and very open about their.. um... Zombie-ness. Where Dr. Phil came from, I am not sure. Maybe the title of the comic made me think of his show.

"ZORPHBERT AND FRED" *Featuring "Melvin" from "Raw Fish"* **by Dawn Griffin**

Written by: Corey Dye   **Comic:** Raw Fish   **URL:** www.drunkduck.com/Raw_Fish
Award-winning "Raw Fish" allows me to say that webcomics gives me some "culture". Corey writes this strip, as an American living in Japan, and shares with us all the weird differences that confuse or amuse him. And yes, his character Melvin has quite the sizeable ears and nose. The Japanese folk must find HIM weird.

"PUT WORDS IN THEIR MOUTHS"
CAMEO PRIZES

"ZORPHBERT AND FRED" *Featuring "The Dude" and other references from "Basketcase"*   by Dawn Griffin

Written by: Kelly Ferguson   **Comic:** Basketcase   **URL:** www.basketcasecomix.com

This one is a bit difficult to explain, but here it goes. Mr. Ferguson creates a 1-panel gag-a-day type comic, which proved to be a challenge for me, as I am used to dealing with mainstay characters. So, instead, I went with his Drunk Duck avatar: a drawing of "The Big Lebowski"'s character "The Dude". His screen name was "Jebus". His comic's name was "Basketcase". Got it now?

"ZORPHBERT AND FRED" *Featuring a plug for "Morning Squirtz" by slimrednina*   by Dawn Griffin

Winner: Dan Mehlhorn   **Comic:** Morning Squirtz   **URL:** www.morningsquirtz.com

Mr. Mehlhorn, another repeat winner, is the co-creator of 2 different webcomics himself. One, aforementioned Slim Red Ninja, is a pimp-tastic action comic, and the other, "Morning Squirtz" is an adult-only hilarious comic with a slew of artists and endless spew-your-coffee jokes you only WISH you could send to your coworkers.

"LEFTOVERS"
DAWN'S FIRST COMIC STRIP

I started "Leftovers" when I was approximately 13-years-old, however it went through several name changes before ending up at "Leftovers" around 1996. It was my baby for over ten years. At 14, I was having my dad neatly xerox pages for syndicate submissions, which I knew would never be truly considered, I mean... I was only a teenager. In fact, in one submission, I blurted out right on the cover page: I AM A TEENAGER. I hoped honesty would at least leave an impression. Not quite. Beyond a few quickly scrawled notes from Jay Kennedy and other comic editors at the bottom of my rejection letters (which I considered my biggest achievement for a while), they were still that: a pile of rejection letters. After ten years, I figured it was time for something new, and I put "The Leftovers"-- a group of modern college grads scraping to get by-- to rest. Here is a sampling of the last submission I mailed off in April 2006.

"THE LEFTOVERS"
DAWN'S FIRST COMIC STRIP

"LEFTOVERS"
DAWN'S FIRST COMIC STRIP

"THE LEFTOVERS"
DAWN'S FIRST COMIC STRIP

"LEFTOVERS"
DAWN'S FIRST COMIC STRIP

"THE LEFTOVERS"
DAWN'S FIRST COMIC STRIP

"LEFTOVERS"
DAWN'S FIRST COMIC STRIP

"THE LEFTOVERS"
DAWN'S FIRST COMIC STRIP

You can purchase the entire collection of "Leftovers" (the syndication submissions, 1994-2004) and other goodies like T-shirts and hats at: **www.cafepress.com/leftoverscomic**

And now, as a conclusion to this book, and because I am apparently a glutton for complete embarrassment, I leave you with my very first comic strip ever (typo included), in the first submission to syndicates.

Dawn Griffin • *age 14* • *circa 1993*

May this be a lesson to you kids: Put your mind to anything, and eventually you won't suck at it.

Made in the USA
Charleston, SC
14 October 2014